Today I Belong to Agnes

Today
I Belong
to Agnes

GLEN SORESTAD

Ekstasis Editions

Canadian Cataloguing in Publication Data

Sorestad, Glen
    Today I belong to Agnes

    Poems
    ISBN 1-896860-73-7

        I. Title.
    Ps8587.O746T62   2000   C811'.54   C00-910490-3
    PR9199.3.S575T62   2000

Acknowledgements:
Earlier versions of some of these poems first appeared in the following literary magazines: *The Dalhousie Review, Dandelion* (25th Anniversary Edition), *Event, The Fiddlehead, Grain, The Nashwaak Review, Poemata, River Review* (U.S.), *The Roswell Literary Review* (U.S.).

    "Hospital Vigil" appeared on the *Read-a-Poem Now* website of The League of Canadian Poets; "Garden Party" first appeared in the anthology, *2000% Cracked Wheat* (Coteau Books, 2000). "Life Gatherings" appeared with a slightly different title in the anthology, *90 Poets of the Nineties* (The Seminole Press, U.S., 1998) and was broadcast on CBC Radio in Saskatchewan, along with several other poems in this volume.

Published in 2000 by:
Ekstasis Editions Canada Ltd.   Ekstasis Editions
Box 8474, Main Postal Outlet   Box 571
Victoria, B.C. V8W 3S1   Banff, Alberta ToL 0Co

THE CANADA COUNCIL | LE CONSEIL DES ARTS
FOR THE ARTS | DU CANADA
SINCE 1957 | DEPUIS 1957

Today I Belong to Agnes has been published with the assistance of a grant from the Canada Council and the Cultural Services Branch of British Columbia.

This book is dedicated to the memory
of Myrtle Tilene Peterson(1906-1998);

and to all the devoted people
who give so much in the care
of those from whom time has
stolen the ability or will
to help themselves.

Contents

III. Hands Reaching

I.

Leavings

Care Assessment

The woman from Home Care talks with Mother,
asks her various questions; Mother proffers
quite credible replies and everything is well
until the assessor asks how old Mother is.
"Oh, I'm a hundred years old," Mother says
without the slightest hesitation; she's eleven years
off the mark this time. "Really? One hundred?"
"Oh, yes," Mother smiles her sweetest affirmation
as the other seeks corroboration in her files.

Now why has Mother decided that today
she will be a hundred years old? Was she
thinking of her favourite aunt who lived
to her hundredth birthday? Has she decided
if her aunt could do it why not she? Or is
Mother engaging in a bit of harmless sport
with this earnest woman, leading her on
before her laughter lets the other know
she's been duped by an eighty-nine year old?

I'm leaning toward the latter when the woman
asks Mother to tell her what time it is. "Why?"
Mother wants to know, "Can't you tell time?"
I sense caginess from Mother that is beyond
the game she may be playing with her opponent.

"Yes, I can. What I want is for you to look
at that clock," and she points at the wall,
"and tell me what time it is right now."
Mother looks at the clock for a few seconds,
then turns to the woman and says, "I don't see
why I should tell you the time, if you can see
the clock perfectly well yourself." Then refuses
to play the match further. But perhaps she knows,
even at this moment, that time has made
an unexpected turn, one she'll not set right,
no matter how she plays the game.

Wrinkles

When she returned from her eye operation,
it was several days before the new lens
restored full vision. Her first concern was
who had been into her apartment
while she was away and had dropped
crumbs and other bits of food on the floor.

When she looked in the mirror
and for the first time noticed how
the operation had aged her,
implanting new wrinkles in her face
along with her new lens,
she was momentarily shocked,
then brought to sudden laughter

and gave her apartment a thorough cleaning.

Thinking

I've been thinking a lot lately,

               Mother says to me one day.

I assure her this is good, thinking is healthy,
but worrying is something to avoid, knowing that all
her life Mother has been a *worry wart,*

                    her self-description.

Oh no, I haven't been worrying,

                 she assures me.
I can't remember anything to worry about!

So I ask her what sorts of things she thinks about
and for a time she doesn't answer and I'm afraid
she's either forgotten the question or her subject.

I've been thinking a lot about Mom and Dad,

                    she says at last
and I know this from previous visits to be true.

I ask her what she remembers of them now;
over a half-century dead, they lie in the country
churchyard where my own father takes his rest.

I don't remember much, but I still think of them lots.
My mother's smile that of a happy child.

Mother vs. Cito

Mother was no sports addict,
but she loved baseball on TV with a passion
that surprised even me. She worshipped
with the congregation of the Blue Jays
as many times a week as there were games.
Her devotion was rewarded with no less
than two World Series championships.

While she loved the Blue Jays as a team,
Cito Gaston embodied the tumult
of her affair with baseball and the Jays.
Mostly she was convinced that Cito
was an planted spy from the hated Yankees,
sent (and no doubt richly rewarded)
by the infamous owner of that franchise.
She believed that Cito was the Blue Jay
Nemesis, not its Manager, whose job
it was to sabotage the best efforts
of the pitching staff by yanking them
when they were pitching well and leaving
them in the game when they were not.

Mother stewed over every Gaston move
and even when her team prevailed in two
successive October showdowns, she was
certain that the team had won despite Cito.
But the Jays became also-rans and Gaston
was swiftly relegated to the refuse heap
where gone-and-forgotten managers languish;
Blue Jay passion died with Cito's going.

She watched games with detachment,
caring little about who won or lost.
Like a fired manager she knew the game
was still being played, the players
performed their feats as before,
but it was going on without her
and could never be the same.

Remote Control

By day Mother uses the remote
to flick, channel to channel;
she can even adjust the volume
when she takes a notion,
though mostly the set blares
and sound fills to overflowing
her small apartment. But these
are the voices that fill her hours,
that fill the void of voices lost.

At bedtime as her mind
unwinds and the time
comes to turn off the TV
she has forgotten what this
unfamiliar black plastic gadget
is for, so she pulls the cord
from the wall socket and
silences the host of speakers.

In the morning she phones me
to come and fix the TV
because it won't come on
and her black gizmo won't work.
The first time this happened
I reviewed with infinite care
and detail the use of the remote,
emphasizing turning off the set.

Next morning I got the same
phone call — and each day
after that. So I quit the review —
after all, she was doing no harm
to herself or the set; and besides,
her confusion turned to serendipity
in uncovering a valid reason
for her son's first visit of the day.

Leavings

In her ninety-first year
my mother experiences mysterious
visitations; she doesn't know
exactly when they come,
perhaps while she dozes
in her chair while TV talk shows
blather without her,
but people come and go,
she's very sure,
leaving behind little things
to confuse her:
costume jewelry, magazines,
old watches, letters and cards,
unfamiliar clothing —
things not there before.

One day she discovers
an entire carton of bedding
the mysterious visitor has left —
sheets and pillow cases she
recognizes enough to know
the house and time.

But now she's discovered
this box, part of the restless
rooting and sorting
that is a prelude to her
final move; it has become
a mysterious leaving
of the unseen one who
comes and goes
through her small rooms
with impunity.

And all she can do is
put her house in order.

Gatherings

It's been weeks, but seems years now
that we've been cleaning Mother's apartment.
Now that she's moved to a private care home
she has no need and less room for all
these possessions that have surrounded her —
reminders of who she is, where she's lived.
At times these comfort objects became puzzles
she'd pick up and stare at: tangible links
to fading times, the confusion of years.

This burden of survival to her tenth decade
is that she sees parts of herself fall away
like dead skin: two husbands, a succession
of homes in different places, two children,
grandchildren, great-grandchildren — all
become many-faceted pieces grown
harder to fit in the jigsaw puzzle
that her life has now become.

But what are we to do with all these things?
At times despair mounts that I must be
the one to decide what shall be kept,
what discarded of this, my mother's life,
part of me in the history of these keepsakes.
Of course, we too have gathered our own,
the incriminating evidence of a lifetime,
plot details of a fiction all too real.
Are we to leave four decades worth
of our own packratting to our children
so that they too must someday
lift and hold each item and agonize
over what has meaning or worth,
what is treasure and what is trash?

II.

Sisterhood

Levels

The care home is
a converted family home
with bedrooms on two levels.

Mother entered as a resident
on the lower floor, then moved
upstairs where those who
need extra attention are
in more constant touch with staff.
Some need help dressing,
some want helping hands to walk;
all need help to bathe. They have
become kindergarten crones
who totter from bedroom
to sitting room to kitchen.

This home allows
for no further levels of attention,
so Mother's options have
already run their course.
Greater care demands
a nursing home: the final
stage in the home
we spend a lifetime building.

Meals

The women are gathered
to the table six times daily
for meals or snacks. It is
not that they require
so many meals a day, but they
would otherwise forget
and often they are here
because they could no longer
remember when to eat.

So in this home the six
daily excursions cast their days
with certainty and ritual,
draw them from naps and TV,
bring them to their feet,
force the blood to flow.
Many of them would
be content to sleep
their time away
but for this.

Table rites become vital
social events; necessary
discourse, not of their own
design, but because they
have lost the pattern.
They are spoken to, reply,
mingle verbally with these
other regulars at the table
whose names they've forgotten.

Each time they move
to another table interlude
it is as if for the first time,
as if a new group is gathered
for some purpose that may
soon become apparent.

Everyman

More than a year, several days a week
I've been a visitor in this care home.
I am so constant the staff anticipates me:
I surprise them only when I do not show.

The residents here have seen me now
so often they can't be sure whether
I am missing husband, son, or brother,
some forgotten family member, or staff.

All they know is that they recognize
my face and I am harmless enough
to be entrusted with family news,
or queried about the latest from home.

I might be a plumber come to fix a tap
for them, electrician or carpet cleaner,
priest or doctor. They do not know
my name; they could call me Everyman.

Birds and Cages

The home's resident budgie is in full throat,
ranting some prolonged refrain that may
or may not be familiar to the assembled ladies.

"Wouldn't it be nice to know what that bird
is going on so about?" one woman asks another.
"Birds shouldn't be in cages," the other replies.

"We had birds in the backyard all winter long,"
says another, "and we kept a feeder for them."
"A feeder? My that must have been nice."

"Peter? Did someone see Peter?" says the one
who has left her hearing aid in her room again.
"I can't hear a thing for that noisy bird!"

Agnes' Album

Agnes brings me her photo album.
I know her only by name. I know
none of her family — a gallery
of perfect strangers. Yet today

Agnes insists I play the role
of family member, attentive as she
haltingly studies first one photo,
then another, summons names

and places from the past, weaves
fragmentary images into a tapestry
of blood and bone that she has lived.
I sit beside her as she speaks.

Her frail voice stumbles as she
seeks in English the words
that would be so easy in Hungarian,
the language of her dreams.

Agnes needs someone to listen
and I am those ears. Though I am
here to visit my mother,
today, I belong to Agnes.

Birthdays

The ladies of the home are at tea, or
coffee, as suits them: their afternoon rite.
Today they're singing someone's birthday, though
whose exactly, none of them can be sure.

As they fork celebratory morsels
to their mouths and slowly chew or swallow,
each of them has fleeting notions it might
be her own. It is a mere flash of sun.

For haven't birthdays always come and gone
with the seasons — children, friends, even theirs?
Here, at this kitchen table, with women
whose names they can't even recall, they share:
teacups and birthday cake, intimate bits,
present and past, time's relentless chorus.

Flirtations

I never overlook an opportunity
for a wee bit of teasing or flirting
on my visits. Not with my mother,
of course — even at her age she sees
through me as mothers always will.

But if one of the ladies is about to sit
on the sofa beside me I always insist
that she behave, to her delight –
feigned surprise aside. Sometimes
I offer to sit on the lap of one
of them for a while — might even
raise a blush and nervous giggle.

We are never too old to be silly,
never too old to be the child,
never too old to wring joy
from the humdrum wash of days.

Flowers

I bring flowers to the home —
a torch of pink carnations
or sunny chrysanthemums
to burnish December dullness,
or a blaze of scarlet begonia
to warm them; and the women
cluster round the floral offering,
drawn as teens to a pizza.

I bring flowers for my mother.
At least I tell myself this.
But I am thinking of them all
each time I bear this burst
of spring and it is not
so selfless an act as it
may seem: does not their
prompt pleasure become mine?

Few of them know my name,
so I am the Flower Man who
splashes their days with a rush
of colour and scent that they
may *oooh* and *aaah*, faces
opening like exotic blooms.

Family Photos

We've given Mother an album —
her children, grandchildren,
even eight great-grandchildren —
labelled all the snapshots,
identified each face fixed
on the page like wood violets
in a childhood scrapbook,
the names that wisp away
like springtime fragrance.

Some days she recognizes
no one; it upsets her — only
while the thought holds.
But she reads the names,
traces letters with her finger,
as though touch might be
the glue to bind these
fragments of her life
in place and keep them
from drifting wherever
names and faces scatter
in their game
of hide-and-seek.

A Cup of Coffee

Every second or third time
I am here to visit Mother
one of the ladies will ask me
if I'd like a cup of coffee.

"I'll put a pot of coffee on,"
says one, but she has no idea
where to find pot or coffee
so she tarries in her chair.

Most of them haven't made
coffee in years; a coffee-maker
an inscrutable mystery.
But unfailing hospitality

remains coded in them, despite
time's slow but certain thievery
and the mind's feeble attempts
to grasp details of the present.

Sometimes I get a cup of coffee
from the staff and each woman
beams and believes it is she
who has been the perfect hostess.

Garden Party

There are four of us sitting on the patio:
Mother, whose short term memory is zero,
another whose mind short-circuits mid-thought,
and the third who is all pragmatism without
a jot of imagination. I am the Mad Hatter
of the group, fuelling conversation
with hints and suggestions. It is either
a Monty Python routine or a Kafka fiction.

"What did you mean by that?"

                              "By what?"

"By your last comment."

                            "What did I say?"

"Don't you remember?"

                            "No, do you?"

There is laughter, not so much because
the humour they are finding is intended,
but it's easier to laugh — and better.
Tears demand comfort and explanations;
laughter needs no justification.

Wisps of intent arise and dissipate
as quickly, unfinished or re-routed
into some nether world of the lost.
The practical one turns to Mother,
asks what the remark by the third means;
but my mother has already forgotten,
so she laughs because they are all
laughing at something none of them
either understands or remembers.
And what better than laughter
to fill the growing silence ?

Hair Care

Once a week, Wednesdays or Thursdays,
a hairdresser appears in the home. Each
woman in turn has a set, or a trim,
sometimes a full perm. It is always
a happy day and each without fail
is surprised and pleased when summoned
to the chair to sit and have the stylist
toss and tease the fine hair
into curls and waves, so that
one by one, each will leave
the chair, metamorphosed
with a bloom of youth,
bursting with the joy of spring.

Territory

In the home the women are
assigned places at the table:
the same place for every meal,
a routine to learn by rote.

This positioning at the table
is a constant, another buffer
against uncertainty and chaos
that lurks outside their doors.

In the livingroom there are no
designated chairs or sofa spots;
in no time they stake their claims
and woe the woman who usurps

the chair another deems hers.
Interlopers may well evoke
accusations and tears. Territory
and its imperative die hard here.

Houses

Some days Mother is convinced this care home
is hers and the other dozen women are here
at her whim or pleasure. They may be amused
or irked, as their own failing minds grapple
with the intricacies of language and intent.

Whenever she is brought up short and told
she does not own the house, nor the table
they all sit around, not even her own room,
she is confused. It doesn't seem right.
Hasn't her son told her this is her home?

She once had a house, maybe more than one ...
Different places, times, have merged and now
she is left with a vague memory of *house*,
something she once owned, but now,
is told is no longer hers, something past.

Some days her house is childhood's farm,
sometimes a small town where she worked
as a cook; at times a tiny bungalow in Burnaby.
Some days *this* house is hers and all houses
have become the one she moves toward.

Memory

My mother has told the other women
that I have not been to see her
for two weeks now. But I was
here just two days ago and brought
along her first cousin; this visit
and many others have disappeared
into some black hole of memory.

She could be angry with me:
dispute facts, call us all liars,
but she accepts failing memory
with humour and grace; it is
easier for us both, though I confess
it hurts to witness, first hand,
what time may hold for me,
should I, too, reach my nineties.

One woman, ninety-seven, corrects Mother:
"Your son was here just two days ago"—
her mind still in step with time-just-past;
she looks forward to spring
so she can sit outside on the deck.
Does some vernal promise nourish
her crisp hold on time, while Mother
languishes in a hazy past peopled by
nameless shadows and blurred faces?

I leave the care home, my presence
already lost. Tomorrow she may complain
she hasn't seen her son for weeks; I know
she will be assured it isn't so and she
will be much more content than I am
as I drive away to the rest of my life.

Missing

For several visits now I have
not seen one of the women –
my mother's closest companion
since both became novitiates
in this house of aged sisters.
I inquire of the missing one,
learn a major stroke has struck
her helpless, relegated her
to a nursing home.

I look at Mother and those
around her. Are they aware
that one of their midst has
left them, never to return?
Do they, for a moment,
when and if the absent one
intrudes upon awareness
think: *there but for*
the grace of God...

Or do they ignore
that empty chair
so the new face that
appears one morning to sit
beside them at breakfast
does not take them by surprise?

The Players

In the home the roster of women
alters little. Line-up changes consist
of deletions followed by additions,
as weakening bodies and minds demand
higher levels of care than the staff
can provide. One day a face
is missing; before long a new
recruit appears and the roster
is back to full complement.

Some go to more intensive care
in nursing homes; others to hospitals
to end their days. Some will draw
their last breath in bed, here
in this home that is not their own,
but somehow is, where they belong
to a ladies' team and all of them
are players in the late innings
of a game where the outcome is
not in doubt, but the game must
be played to the final at bat.

Language

Mother struggles to express herself.
She begins to say something,
then a word refuses to emerge
from the sewing bag of language
and she gropes for what eludes her
until the thread of intent snaps
and her idea falters, disappears
into the discard heap of beginnings
and seams of unfinished sentences.

But when her cousin greets
her in Norwegian, first language
of childhood chatter, she threads
words with dexterity, while
the second language weakens.
In her ear now are the voices
of her long-dead parents calling, calling.

Musical Interlude

I open the door to unexpected
rough-edged fiddle sound, accordion
and acoustic guitar: an old dance
melody in full swing. The reel

(or is it a jig, I can't tell)
swirls up the carpeted steps
from the basement level
to the ladies of the parlour.

They sit in their usual places,
eyes closed, most of them;
they could be asleep, but for
the palpable tapping of feet,

the slight movement of lips
as a tune stirs forgotten lines.
Downstairs three aging musicians,
slowed fingers now groping

once-familiar stops, transform
the home to Saturday dancehall
where each woman awaits a turn
to dance in the arms of the past.

Naps

Mother naps more often now,
though if asked she's quick to deny.
Most visits, I find her dozing
in a livingroom chair, slumped
into the privacy of slumber.

She is in good company,
surrounded by her colleagues
of the afternoon snooze.
Like nursery pre-schoolers,
after cookies and juice they nap,

some with mouths agape,
softly purring in peace;
some with heads thrown back
in purposeful bliss, others
cocooned in deep secrets.

They all nap more, glide
into the guilelessness of sleep
with neither apology nor pretence,
content to let the world resolve
its problems without them.

New Furniture

One of the resident ladies says to me:

I've just bought some new furniture.
Did you notice?

        And her hand
in a flourish embraces the living room
and the chesterfield suite that has been
in place since long before she came here.
None of the other women offers
to dispute her claim, though what
each thinks or whether it has
even registered is not easy to read.

There's no point telling her this house
does not belong to her. At least she's
comfortable enough in her circumstances
to believe, if only for the moment,
in this care home as her very own.

Yes, you've made a very good choice.
The colours suit the room just right,

                       I say.

Night Relief

When I ask the woman on duty
why there is no waste container
on the floor of Mother's room
for the discarded paper tissue
I have just used to help her
attend to her runny nose,

I am told the staff often
has to remove the containers
from the rooms to prevent
the residents from using them
to urinate in at night.

My dumbfounded stare prompts
her to explain: when they
awaken in the night they seldom
know where they are, or where
the bathroom is, and may even
be in some house of childhood,
remembering privy buckets
or bedpans or thundermugs.

But when nocturnal urgency
of weakening bladders calls,
ingenuity is not long to reply.

Ninety-nine and Counting

Today is Dorothy's birthday:
she is ninety-nine, her mind still
keen with detail of time and place.
She snuffs the single candle
with quick and easy grace,
accepts accolades, birthday wishes,

then lifts her head, purses
her lips with satisfied grit
and says to no one in particular:
    Tomorrow, I shall begin
    my one hundredth year...

A simple assertion as if
she were informing us
she was going for a nap,
not making a pronouncement,
or prediction of the future —
a moment of indulgence which,
on this occasion we embrace.

Parents

The first time Mother asks me
how her parents are doing,
I am taken aback, not sure
how to answer, but I recognize
she dwells in time before me.
When I tell her they've been gone
now over fifty years, she's shocked.
I have jolted her from a place
where she was surrounded by
siblings and parents and love.

Next visit she repeats the query
and each visit now I have to tell her
that her mother and father are dead;
each time her surprise is genuine.
She awakens daily to a younger world
and in this realm I, nor anyone who
follows me, do not exist: I am only
a curious visitor who comes to talk.

One day her childhood cousin is with
when Mother asks the question.
Her cousin tells her they've been gone
a long, long time, but that both
she and Mother will be seeing them
before too long. Mother is content.
Her eighty-nine year old cousin
could say what I had neither
courage nor sense to offer.

Pension Cheques

One resident claims the oddest
moment in her life was the day
her daughter came to show her
she, too, was now receiving
old age pension. She says
she was shocked; never had it
occurred it could be possible.
They both found it so ludicrous
they laughed until they cried.

The woman says it was hard
accepting that both of them could
be senior citizens at the same time.
And now that her twin sons have
turned sixty-five, she finds
her entire family on the pension.

But how can children possibly have
this same status as their parents?
It lingers as a mind-boggler
her head can't work its way around.
The best thing to do is laugh.

Sideways World

My mother, at ninety, become rebel.

She cultivates a fondness
for leaning to one side or the other
in the easy chair or on the sofa
until her head slips nearly parallel
to the floor. She prefers to watch
TV from this unique perspective
and when I ask whether she
would like me to help her
regain uprightness, she chuckles
and says it's all the same,
no matter how you look at it.

The staff claim if you straighten her
she soon resumes her skewed view,
so they've opted to grant her
this eccentric glimpse of life.

I suppose I could insist that she
be more closely supervised and be
compelled to regard life squarely,
head-on, to share the collective sight
of the vertical in a horizontal world,
but secretly I rather relish the notion
of my mother at ninety turning rebel,
an anarchist to boot, she who lived
nine decades of beholding life
through straight-ahead spectacles.

My mother, at ninety, twisting
the world sideways
to get a second opinion,
resisting the efforts of all,
even her own son, to return her
to the safe conformity of the masses.

My mother, at ninety, a mutineer —
that pleases me. It gives me hope.

Sisterhood

At first I thought, how sad,
how tragic — to look around
this gathering of aged women,
this sisterhood of survivors,

but this sombre view was
mine alone. For when I
cleaned my glasses I observed
contentment in every face —

perhaps not always, but they
were children of a family
and though most could not
name their new siblings,

they knew with mysterious
certainty they belonged.
The sadness was mine,
the sadness of the blind.

Snapshots

Gina brings a double set of prints to show —
family photos, a life she lived in a prairie town
before her memory began its certain shutdown
and her present dissipated in Alzheimer's fog.

She talks me through both sets, not once
realizing she repeats each moment. One print
a tiny white frame house, hers, she remembers,
but is puzzled by the rooftop TV antennae,

thinks this must be a bird feeder they erected.
When she concludes her impromptu show-and-tell,
a double colour print journey through her past,
she unknowingly begins anew and now

the story alters shape and one she identified
as her brother becomes someone new whose name
she can't recall, the white house now her brother's
and in this telling located in another province.

In vain she struggles to retain her own story,
faces and places that each day fade closer to loss.
In time these photographs will no longer be
her life at all, just lifeless bits of gloss.

Sundays

As I am talking to Mother,
one of the other women
comes to sit beside me
and asks who I am here
to see. She has seen me
every time I come,
but for her the immediate
past has been stolen
and I am new to her
each time I arrive.
She asks if someone
has a birthday today
because there are so
many visitors around.
I tell her the reason is
it's Sunday — and she smiles.

"Oh yes," she says, "Sunday."
She smiles as she considers,
"I think that's when I get
a visit from my son.
Do you think he'll come?"

"I would expect so," I reply.

"What day is it today, anyway?"

Television Afternoon

Of all the programs, the cooking shows
appear to interest and amuse the ladies most.
No Jerry Springer brawling spouses,
but rather, chefs in white, tossing pizza dough,
or stuffing pale fillets of sole with concoctions
of mushrooms or tiny shrimp with cheese;
they are impressed with fancy knife-work
on the chopping block, love the colours
of paellas or pilafs, and ragouts and jambalayas.

They loll back in their chairs or sofas,
snooze during the commercials and beyond,
but focus on ingredients as if committing
the recipes to recall, though it has deserted them.
Even soundless, the cooking shows still win
over the afternoon soaps and talkfests,
as soups are stirred and bread is baked, a leg
of lamb festooned with cloves of garlic,
red bell peppers stuffed with Basmati rice,
a decadence of chocolate drizzled over pears
poached in Gewurtztraminer, the mute chefs
smiling and gesturing, holding up each
newly garnished plate to the camera —
and to the ladies, who withhold applause
like Russian skating judges, but who
sometimes betray appreciation with smiles
measured with memory and knowing.

.

Woman in Sleep

Who can say how
old this woman is,
but whatever the age
she is by choice or design
sleeping her days away,
as if somehow her life
has been a prolonged chore
from which at last
she is freed.

She must be awakened
for medicine or meals,
her ill-tempered petulance
unseemly in one otherwise
so silent, an ancient fetus
curled beneath her blanket,
dreaming details left undone.

This tiny covered crumple
may have perished
the precise second she lifted
her fingers from the last task
and now this inert heap
of fragile bones and slowing
blood is far distanced
from the one who drove
her days to drudgery
in another time,
in another place.

Transients

The woman with Alzheimer's says she's just visiting,
though she's been here several months or more.
She insists she's just here until she goes home.

She has no idea where she is, except she has
a room with objects that have meaning, though
on any day one of them might become new,

as memory and purpose escape and then resurface
like puzzle pieces hidden by an impish child.
Though she is younger than her tablemates,

she and all of us are simply transients, stopping
here awhile to catch our breaths before our travel
leads us to the next sojourn, or our final destination.

Visitors

1.

Each Thursday the tall
immaculate man arrives
without fail to visit
his mother, but only
Thursdays.

Newly retired he now
looks for meaning in life
without work,
an organization man
who has lived
a structured life
and will never
bend to chaos.

Still, I'd like to ask
him why it must be
Thursday only;
his mother would
be pleased to see him
any day, frequency
would do no harm,
especially since her days
are swiftly moving
to that moment when
one Thursday she
will no longer give
his afternoon its purpose
and the neat order
of his week will
collapse upon him.

2.

This woman must be a school teacher
because she wants to scold her mother:

Sit up straight now! Where's your hankie?
Tuck in your blouse! Are you listening?

Is this a daughter's revenge on her mother?
Must it come to this? The daughter can

not help herself, it seems. No matter how
warm her greetings, no matter how much

or little they may have to say to each other,
at some point the visit always comes to this.

Perhaps it is a kind of love, the only kind
these two have ever known, or ever shown.

3.

One woman visits her mother often
and each time the visit ends in tears,
not because one has offended the other,
but because each time they part it is
as if it could be for the very last time;
their hearts well up and overflow.
Each parting leaves no guarantee
of future meetings; instead each
leaving brings them closer to pain,
the emptiness of silence after tears.

4.

Each time this woman comes
she works so hard to hide
how her mother's falling back
to childhood upsets her —
as if somehow this should
not be so, as if someone here
must be responsible for
what she sees happening.
She is not yet ready
to see herself
in her mother's place,
refuses to see
what each of us must see.

Weather

Thelma always asks the same question:
"Is it very cold outside?" Or else,
a variation: "Is it nice out there?"

She sits beside the window,
sunlight splashing her
frail shoulders and quavers,

"Is it very cold outside?"
I assure her the weather's fine,
return my attention to Mother.

Thelma is going nowhere today,
so weather is nothing more
than a gambit for attention.

"Is it very cold outside?"
she quakes again — the former
question and answer lost.

This plaintive refrain
is a tiring constant and
at times it tries my patience,

but I answer each tremulous
query as though it were
the first, as though I could

bring sunny days to gardeners,
or timely showers to farmers.
I bring Thelma the weather.

Women Without Men

They have lived much of their lives
with men and now in their final years
they are partnerless survivors.
Some linger in grief and regret
for lovers gone; some cheer
in dark silence their release
from bonds of fear;
some have forgotten those
who shared their beds,
who shared their lives.

Here, in their eighties and nineties
they are a random company:
ancient crones living with memories,
sometimes fleeting and faint,
sometimes sharp with longing,
memories of time when there was
an other, a presence that this place
can not evoke, that this home
of aged strangers have in common
but can never truly share.

Mini-Strokes

Some days I can see
perceptible changes in Mother,
or in one of her companions:
a tangible faltering of speech,
a sudden memory gap,
an unsteadiness that wasn't
there the day before.

Her body is under attack
from within, tiny assaults
that day by day move her
towards a final surrender;
the body is untraining itself
in some natural regression
to infancy, to diapers
and the mewl of the newborn.

Dreamers

It is night and the house
is filled with sleep.
In every bed, every room
women lost in dream.

In one room a sleeper
holds a doll received
on her fifth birthday,
Eaton's very finest.

Across the hall another
feels two strong arms holding
her close and she cries out
the name of her loss.

One dreams of shelling peas
fresh picked in a July garden,
while her neighbour walks
sticky-mouthed at the fair.

A farm wife dreams a dog
chasing cows from the wheat;
another is eavesdropping
on the rural party phoneline.

One dreams a favourite uncle,
killed in the trenches at Vimy;
another shrinks and curls herself
at the fierce hand of her father.

In every room slumber dramas
spin through the darkness
like silent films, reel by reel,
the house a mute theatre.

Home

Mother wants to go home. She tells me this
and I ask where I am to take her. *Home.*

This is your home now, I tell her. *Look, here
is your room, your bed, your clothes...*

I have confused her. The objects are familiar,
they are part of her. Comfort, this private space.

Her mind circles to the same troubling image:
When will you be taking me home?

I want to pose the question as kindly as I can,
But where is home now, Mother? She can't say.

I suppose she looks to me for answers now,
not questions. I could speak of her final home,

but I don't think this is what she has in mind,
though perhaps it does lurk on the margins.

But what does this word evoke now for her?
At ninety-one what is the shape of *home*?

III.

Hands Reaching

Stroke

When the stroke that is the beginning of the end comes there is no way of knowing that it is both a beginning and an ending: it is the beginning of the loss of will, the loss of drive that keeps the body upright, moving against time. It is an ending of this woman as we know her, an ending of life for her as she has lived it, an ending that augurs yet another ending. The stroke catches us all off-guard, Mother as much as any of us; she is suddenly weak, hesitant, loses bladder control, no longer able to stand or move on her own. All this in a heartbeat. A sudden coursing of the blood. One moment, one snap of the fingers, from a modicum of independence to total dependency. She puts on her bravest face, relies on humour to feed her, comfort us, but the spark has died. It's gone from her eyes, from her voice, from her whole being, this once-robust woman who nourished me in her womb now become frail and helpless, barely able to raise herself in her hospital bed. After ninety-two years the fuel that fired her spirit is all but spent.

Hospital Vigil

I stand beside her bed,
watch her withered body
rise and fall in fitful sleep

and it is hard. This body
on the bed is not my mother;
my mother has already gone.

This is just a dying woman,
a body to fill the hours
of the doctors and nurses,

a body to fill the charts
with data to analyze
and cost out in dollars,

statistics for the health
of the health care system.
My mother is already gone,

though this covered shape
on the bed rises and falls,
rises and falls, rises and falls.

Wheelchairs

The stroke that hospitalizes Mother
dictates a move to another home —
from private care with its minimal
but essential veil of independence
to extended care, a nursing home.

On my first visit to her new quarters
I step through the front doorway
into a wagon train of wheelchairs,
drawn together in the rotunda,
a circle of covered wagons
preparing for a hostile assault —
silent and stoic as they await
the slings and arrows.

A few of them size me up,
dismiss me as harmless, so I
traverse the gauntlet unscathed.
Before I can find the room
where Mother is, I am
overwhelmed by wheelchairs,
gleaming chrome everywhere,
motionless, or creeping toward
some meandering aim.
Weakened limbs granted reprieve
by silent rubber wheels.

As I stride past rolling chairs
and eyes fixed on distant goals
I am self-conscious of movement,
my muscles, ligaments and bones
in easy motion, blood coursing
through my body, my whole being
in an accustomed healthy stride,
moving through this near-stasis,
the relentless wheeling of time.

Activity Director

She wants to talk to me about
Mother's interests — her voice
amiable, the happy mask of one
still in love with her work.

What interests a dying woman?
I want to ask her this.
*Can't you see that all she wants
to do right now is leave —*

*not just this building and all
who flutter to and fro —
but me, you, every one of us?
She no longer wants to live.*

But this young woman brims
noble intent, sincere desire:
she wants to bring some joy
to the dying of her patients,

so how can I not acquiesce
to her request and meet her
on her terms — at least
while Mother is still here?

Losing Speech

In her ninety-second year
my mother is losing ability
to converse. Increasingly words
elude her, and the originating
thought hides while
she seeks the word.
Conversation now is
a series of opening fragments.
Beginnings become entireties,
remnants of intent. She is
now unlearning language.
Memory, the storehouse
of vocabulary and idiom,
is well into deconstruction;
the tongue falters, turns
sluggish as use lessens
in this inevitable,
this painful
journey into silence.

Care Dog

The care home dog pads from one
woman to the next; each brief stop
evokes a pat on the head, a stroke,
endearing words, low murmurs.

The dog answers to as many names
as there are women in the home;
yet it knows with animal sureness
not one of these is its own.

Each day the dog performs its role
as object of affection for each
of these now left alone, for whom
this brief touch triggers memory

and the dog reminds them anew
of pets and people that still live
in misty mornings of life past.
The dog betrays nothing of this.

Like dreams the dog comes and goes,
stirring in each one that leans
to ruffle its coat, pet its head,
twinges of the unforgotten.

Hands Reaching

It's better if you don't take their hands,
the helpful young woman informs me,
then you won't have the problem
of dealing with them
when you want to leave.

Residents hunched in their chairs
extend gnarled hands, veins raised
like cordillera relief maps, call out
to me as I pass. They don't know me,
the name uttered, indistinguishable,
but I am someone in their past
they would like to talk with,
perhaps a touch remembered
and desired again as no other.

It's better if you don't make eye contact
with them, she adds. *It just encourages them.*
I know she is trying to help me
to avoid moments that have recurred
ad infinitum in her days on staff —
the embarrassed visitors besieged
by nameless elderlies who clutch
and clamber like the capsized. But part
of me is appalled; part of me wants
to stop, take each reaching hand,
stroke that hand and speak
those words we all desire.
The other part of me obeys the staff,
walks past the wavering hands,
past the clamour of voices that call,
and call long after I leave.

The Day Mother Doesn't Know Me

Mother speaks to me in generalities,
guarded in her answers
when I ask what she has been doing;
at last I realize that she is
speaking to a stranger who wants
her to confide in him things
he has no right to know.

I am her son
and now for the first time
since she bore the pain of my arrival
howling into this life, she has
rejected me as a prying busybody;

then I prick the balloon
of my silly self-image enough
to know that this is just
the first time it will happen

and there is nothing either of us
can do about it. We are players
in a drama neither has written.
There's no way to change our lines.

What Keeps Us Going

With the arrival of each baby boy,
seven great-grandsons in succession,

Mother expressed equal joy for each,
while desire for a baby girl burned.

The long awaited great-granddaughter
arrived three weeks before Mother died.

By this time she often failed
to recognize me, though I visited her

several times each day. She could hear
Death tapping his foot in the next room;

her will to persevere had died sometime
in the weeks of doctors and hospital beds.

But the birth of the baby girl rallied her,
so that nurses kept repeating this news

daily to raise her spirits, if only for a moment
before the event faded into the mystery

of forgotten names and faces of her life,
while Death cleared his throat and tapped...

The Night My Mother Died

What I remember now
was how she slipped away
so quietly, without fanfare,
the way she lived her life —
no drama, no blinding lights
to set the eyelids aflutter,
no least flicker of recognition
that she saw the brilliant stairs
that marked her passage,
no last deep indrawn Oh!
Nothing. She stopped breathing.

I watched all her life fall
back into the dark cave that was
her open mouth, taking with it
my first squall and all six decades
of my life, all collapsed and falling
into the mystery of her leaving
and the void in all the places
she had been, the greatest
of these voids in me.

The Bones at Rest

My mother's cousin is the family memory.
Precise dates and years roll from her tongue —
pre-recorded arrival and departure times
of the ancestral airline. She is keeper
of our collective past, the family tree grown
inside her head, its roots spread down
through her veins and arteries to the soles
of her feet. She is rooted in our history,
knows its length and breadth, its triumphs
and its failures, moments of jubilation
balancing the teeter-totter with despair.

Before her the tree rooted in her mother
and when death came, the mind no longer
able to encompass a century of births and deaths,
the whole repository flowed into her daughter
and endured. But now she, too, grows old,
and in her late eighties, childless, knows
no one can lift from her the weight of memory.
When she dies the tree inside will perish,
leaves drop one by one, roots decay as she
too must to grow the little patch of grass
in the country graveyard of her kin.

"Ancestors are tiny bones that catch in the throat"

— David Johnson